Book Descriptio[n]

The Trading Bible contains secrets that the top traders don't want to reveal. In this book, we will discuss the working strategies and the dos and don'ts of trading from A-Z, so you can start trading the right way and never lose your money again. This book contains a group of methods that have been approved by the best traders in the world, as well as information that every trader (or aspiring trader) needs to know before entering this wonderful industry.

Throughout this book, you will learn all the necessary techniques to properly invest in the best financial assets, such as stocks, crypto, commodities, and forex. Also, you will find relatable information that can be used in real life, not like other books that give the reader easy to comprehend information that can't be used in their life.

This book will also teach you to protect yourself from all those scammers who try to take advantage of less experienced people in financial terms, and thus deceive them to keep their money. The Trading Bible contains every single detail a person should know to start trading operations, as well as the key to becoming a profitable long-term trader. Without a doubt, this book is made for all those people who want to learn deeply about these topics and take definitive control of their finances, so as not to depend on a salary or work ever again.

The Trading Bible: A-Z about Trading for Beginners and Experts

---

The Authoritative Guide on How to Trade Like a Pro

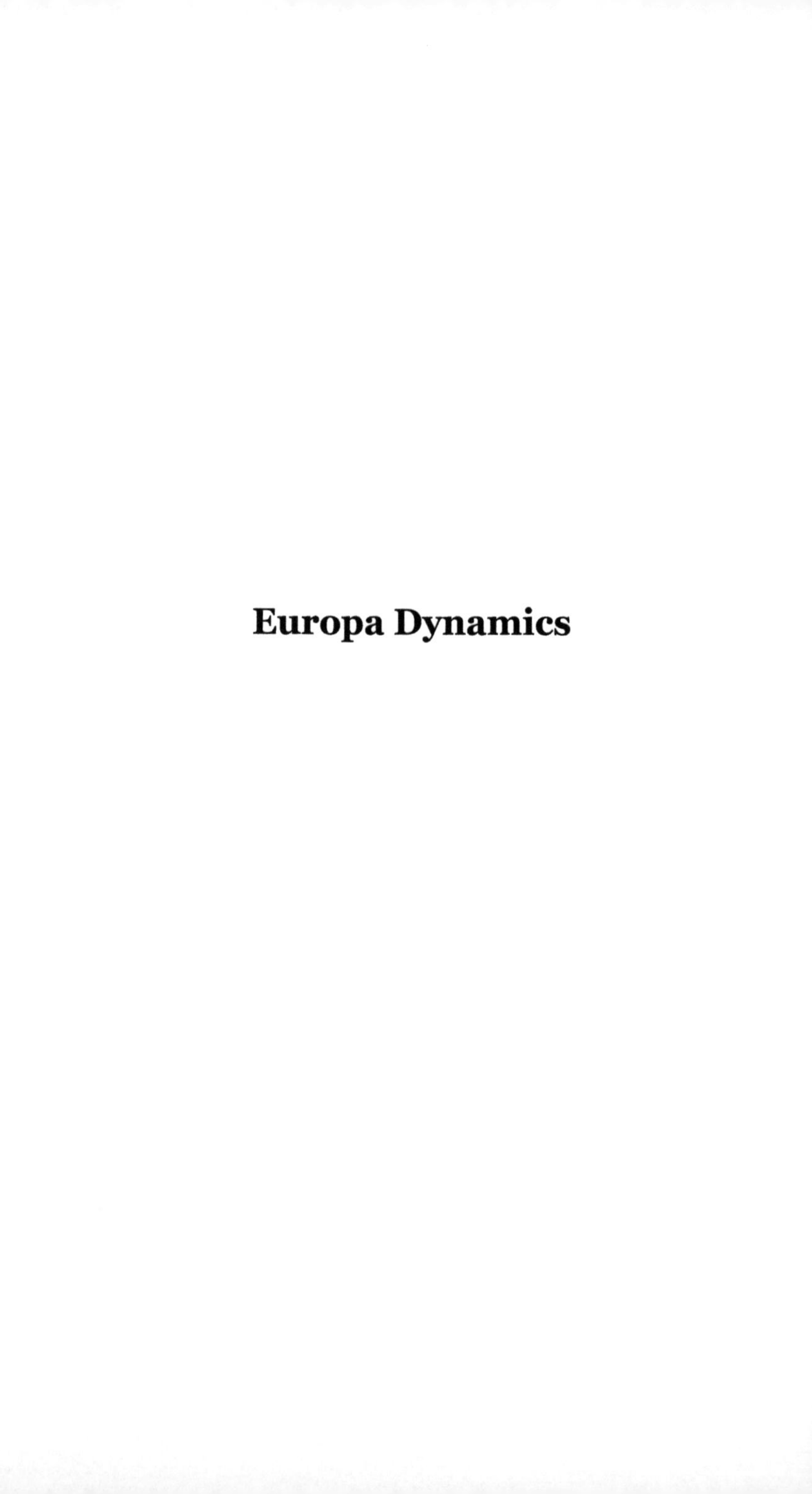

Europa Dynamics

Table of Contents

Introduction

Many people spend their entire lives trying to improve their economic situation and achieve financial freedom; however, very few people do. This is not because it is an impossible task or because it is something that is reserved for people from high society, but it is because people do not know all the methods and strategies that they can use to earn money from the comfort of their home without making any physical effort. While this is not as easy as it seems, it does require knowledge and, of course, a high level of discipline and effort.

One of those highly effective methods to generate money from our own homes is trading. This activity is available to everyone, but unfortunately many people do not take advantage of it since they believe that they must have a lot of knowledge in the area of economics and finance. The truth is that trading is an extremely effective investment tool, and if we know how to take advantage of it, we can use it to start building generational wealth. That is why, throughout this book, you will discover all the secrets to be successful in trading, as well as identify those false mentors who often want to play with people's inexperience and offer them courses and very expensive advice, which end up being ineffective.

Unlike previous times, today we only need a computer or smartphone and an internet connection to be able to carry out trading operations. This means that we do not have to be in a specific country, a sophisticated office, or a specialized place on Wall Street to be able to take advantage of all the great things that this investment tool offers us. Without a doubt, if we educate ourselves with the right techniques and gather the necessary knowledge, we can start multiplying our savings and even make a lot of extra money in our free time through trading. That is another great advantage offered by this activity. It does not matter if we do not want to become full-time traders, since we can do it as a supplementary activity to our main job, as a way to obtain a side income that helps us pay our monthly bills, or simply, as a fun new hobby to enjoy any way we want.

Of course, trading should not be taken as a game either, as our precious money is at stake. That is why we must educate ourselves as best as possible before we start investing our money in this type of activity. If we start investing solely based on speculation or basing our operations on the news that we see on television or in the newspapers, then the chances that we can be successful in trading will decrease dramatically.

Once we begin to delve even further into the wonderful world of trading, we will realize that it is not only an activity that will allow us to multiply our money but that it will also provide us with many hours of entertainment and adrenaline. Without a doubt, this is an excellent activity to improve our economic situation (no matter what it is) and begin to take full control of our finances, to start walking down the road in search of the long-awaited financial freedom.

Chapter 1: The Start of Your Trading Journey

Without a doubt, the world of trading is super interesting and, of course, very profitable. There are very few tools that will allow us to generate money in such a comfortable way since we are free to choose the place where we are going to do it. First of all, we must define what trading is. Generally, the definition of commercial exchange is given, where a buyer and a seller trade the sale of a financial asset, which can be a stock of a company, crypto, currency, commodity contracts, futures, or any of the many options available in the stock market.

Unlike a traditional sale, in trading, it is not necessary to make a formal contract or any of the things that are done when, for example, a real estate property or vehicle is sold. Instead, trading occurs 100% online, and millions of operations are performed around the world daily. Some traders dedicate themselves full time to carry out this type of operation, while other people do it partially, intending to have a side income that helps them increase their monthly income. That is why trading is not only an excellent financial tool, but if we do it the right way, it can solve many of our financial problems.

The ABC of a Trader

Trading is not a difficult activity to do, and that is why, despite what many believe, it is not necessary to have a university degree in finance or a career related to economics. Trading (and the stock market in general) is an investment mechanism that is open to anyone who wants to take advantage of it. Of course, this does not mean that it is extremely simple, since we must have the correct preparation so as not to lose our money.

All traders (regardless of whether it is an experienced trader or a person who simply wants to have a side income) must have a lot of discipline if they really want to be successful in trading. Also, every trader needs specific knowledge that we will expose in this book in order to be able to build their own trading plan.

One of the main things to do before starting to trade in the market is to put together a trading plan. This plan must detail everything related to the trading activities that we are going to carry out, such as how many hours we will do it per day, how much money we will invest weekly, in which financial assets we are going to invest, in which market we should enter and all the other personal aspects that we must consider. This plan will mark our tasks for each day, so that we have a step-by-step guide to guide us on the way.

The Winning Lines

After we have put together our trading plan, we must take into account certain practical aspects of trading. One of the most important things to be mindful of is the support and resistance lines. These lines are like the oxygen of the traders. That is to say, they cannot live without them. The support line indicates the price at which a financial asset has remained above and the price the asset has not fallen below. On the other hand, the resistance line is the opposite, since it indicates the price at which the asset has not been able to overcome.

In the same way, it is important to use the lines of the minimum points and the maximum points. To obtain these lines, we must draw a diagonal line that passes through all the minimum points in which the price of the asset has fallen in a certain period of time, and then do the same but with the maximum peaks that the price has had. After drawing these lines, we can have a clearer picture of where the asset price is heading, so that we can choose whether to make a call put option (also known as buy and sell).

Trading works through these two options, and it is about being able to predict where the price of the financial asset will go using the aforementioned tools. When we make a call or buy option, it is because we believe that the price of that asset will go up, while when we make a put or sell option it is because we believe that the price of the asset will go down. These are the basic options of trading, and it is the way in which money is made through this mechanism. If we know how to use these lines of analysis, we can have a much more solid base on which to decide what kind of operation we should carry out.

How to Start Trading with an

Online Broker

It is highly recommended that novice traders start their operations in demo accounts, also known as paper trading accounts. These accounts allow people to trade fake money in markets with real quotes. This will help us practice in the market, and when we are ready to start investing with real money, we must open a live trading account.

Currently, there are many highly recommended and certified online brokers, such as Robinhood, TD Ameritrade, Webull, Stash, and Acorns, where we can open an account quickly, easily, and for free. Most of these online brokers offer the advantage that they do not charge any commission, so we can make the amount of daily trades we want without having to worry about additional costs.

Most of these online brokers only request that we provide some personal information such as our full name, a photo of an identity document such as our passport or driver's license, and our tax identification number. With this data, we will be ready to trade and start making money from wherever we are (as long as we do it in a responsible and disciplined way). It is always recommended that we only use financial brokers that are certified by the Securities and Exchange Commission (SEC) so that our money is not in danger.

Chapter 2: The Best Options

There are various types of financial assets in which you can invest and perform various trading operations. The choice of the financial asset that we are going to choose will depend solely on our tastes and objectives, since there is not one that is better than the other. Because of this, it is highly subjective. Of course, below, we will see the main characteristics of each, so that we have the necessary information to choose which financial asset is best for us.

Trading Stocks

Historically, stocks have been the most traded financial asset in the world of trading. This refers to the shares that companies make available so that any investor or trader around the world can buy or operate with them. In fact, a large part of the stock market is made up of stocks, and these are the most chosen by long-term traders or investors, but it is not the most favorite for those traders who carry out their operations in the short term.

This is mainly because stocks are not as volatile in the short term as other financial assets. That means that the price does not tend to change as quickly as other assets such as crypto or Forex. However, stocks are used in the stock market as a long-term investment option, since their price tends to increase over time. Therefore, value investors, like growth investors, prefer stocks for their long-term operations, and day traders or other short-term traders tend to use other assets such as crypto, the foreign exchange market (better known as forex), or binary options.

This means that, if we are traders with long-term objectives, without a doubt we must look for the stocks of the different companies available in the market in order to operate successfully. Of course, if we are day traders, it is possible that we will prefer some other financial assets with much more volatility in order to take advantage of the sudden movements in price and to be able to carry out different daily operations that allow us to earn money.

Time for Crypto

Since its creation in 2010, cryptocurrencies have been one of the financial assets with the most unknowns on the market. This is because nothing is even known about its creator, since it was founded anonymously by a person who participated in an amateur investor forum. One of the greatest attractions of crypto is that they are fully decentralized, which is why they are not regulated or controlled by a central bank or the government, unlike currencies such as the dollar or the euro.

A huge increase has been seen in traders trading crypto, especially bitcoin and Ethereum, as they are highly volatile financial assets and can generate staggering returns in no time. However, we must be very careful when carrying out operations that involve crypto, since many times the volatility can be so abrupt that we could have huge losses. Similarly, there is currently very little information about most cryptocurrencies, and they are characterized by having a too sensitive demand. This means that any news or novel event involving a crypto could generate incredible movements in the price.

Without a doubt, if we are going to invest in crypto, we have to make sure that we do as much research as possible about the currency with which we are conducting our financial operation.

If we are not sure what is causing the movements in the price of that currency or if we see that there are strange movements in demand, it is better that we do not do operations at that time, since the market can be extremely unstable, which is very dangerous for beginning traders.

Don't Forget about Commodities

Similarly, certain commodities such as gold, silver, sugar, wheat, and even water are often used to carry out trading operations. Of course, it is not necessary that we materially buy any of these products, but we can carry out trading operations based on the future price of each of these commodities.

In order to operate successfully in this specific market, it is necessary that we study the supply and demand of the specific commodity with which we are going to operate. This information is widely available on the web, and it is necessary to analyze it in order to establish operations with a foundation and not based on speculation. Similarly, we must bear in mind that supply and demand can be strongly affected by certain situations or external factors, such as government decisions, natural disasters, macroeconomic or social situations.

Forex, OTC, and Other Markets

Likewise, there are also other quite popular options with which you can operate in the market, such as forex and over the counter markets (OTC). All these options are highly volatile, since the operations are usually carried out based solely on the speculation of the traders, since there is not much information on which to base the respective analysis.

The foreign exchange market, or forex, consists of carrying out operations based on the variation of the price of one currency over another. For example, a trader can make a trade in the dollar currency pair on the euro, where he will take advantage of the instantaneous volatility and the high flow of operations to enter and exit the market quickly. For its part, OTC refers to operations in markets that are not governed by a specific schedule, which means that it is available 24 hours a day. Also, the OTC market offers some financial assets that are not traded in bigger exchanges.

However, we must be very careful if we are going to operate in either of these two markets, since there is not much information to make solid decisions based on some type of analysis. On the other hand, these types of operations are usually carried out solely based on technical analysis—that is, analyzing the price charts and studying the movements of supply and demand, something that is certainly not recommended for traders without much experience.

Chapter 3: A Guide to Build Wealth in Trading

Trading can be an extremely beneficial tool in economic terms, as long as it is done the right way. Many people are carried away by the comments of some people who claim that they have become millionaires in a short time through trading, in order to sell their supposedly educational courses or other information or subscription material. However, it is very difficult for a person to become rich through trading in a short time, since it is a process similar to that of a snowball, meaning you have to accumulate profits little by little and not get carried away by emotional decisions that can cause us to lose money.

There are some methods that can help a trader organize how they would operate in the market. The most used are day trading and long-term trading, also known as positional trading. Both approaches are totally valid, only that the most suitable for us will depend on our objectives. So basically, it will depend on if we want to generate money in the short term but with a little higher risk involved or if we want our profits to be accumulated in the long term with a slightly lower level of risk.

The Basics of Day Trading

Day trading is one in which people open and close their positions on the same day, so they can perform several operations at once. However, this also carries quite a high risk, since that person could end up losing a lot of money in just one day. That is why we must be very cautious if we are going to choose day trading as the preferred way of doing operations in the market.

Similarly, there are not many possibilities to analyze a possible choice in day trading. This happens because unlike positional trading (which is long-term) we must make extremely fast decisions, which often causes us not to evaluate our options in the best way. That is why we can conclude that if we want to generate multiple short-term profits, we should consider this type of approach to carry out our operations. On the other hand, if what we really want is to build wealth in the long term, it is better that we take other types of approaches, such as positional trading.

Benefits Of Long-Term Trading

Long-term trading has many advantages. One of the main benefits of this approach is that we have many more tools to be able to analyze our operations. This is because, if we are going to carry out operations with stocks, we can evaluate the income statements of the companies and all the other financial balances. If we are going to carry out operations with crypto, we can evaluate how supply and demand have been in recent months, as well as the news that surrounds each of those currencies. None of this can be done in short-term trading, since there is no time to do that kind of analysis, which makes the basis of our decisions very difficult, since they will be based much more on speculation.

Likewise, long-term trading has a great advantage over all other trading approaches, as it allows traders to be able to make corrections in the middle of their operations. This means that, if a trader performs a good analysis, it does not matter what the momentary volatility does, since, being a long-term operation, it will only matter how it ends and not how it begins. On the other hand, in regard to short-term trading, if a trade is affected by volatility at a certain time, it could end up generating heavy losses, since there is not enough time for the market to make any correction.

Focus on Generational Wealth

Many people start in the world of trading because they want to become millionaires overnight, and the truth is that this is something that is almost impossible to achieve in trading, because success can't be achieved overnight in the finance world. Instead, our true goal should be to become profitable long-term traders, in order to accumulate large profits and build generational wealth.

If we know how to manage our operations in the best way, we can earn a significant amount of money in the long term, and best of all, we can do it consistently. There are very few other industries in which we can achieve this, since there are not many areas that allow us to generate money from our home and be able to accumulate large income in a relatively simple way, since there is no physical effort involved in trading. Of course, this does not mean that it is a simple activity. On the contrary, it actually takes a lot of discipline and dedication to become a truly successful trader, but without a doubt, we can achieve it if we put our mind to it and work hard enough.

Chapter 4: Be Aware of the Scams

Every day, we see more and more people becoming interested in the world of trading. However, many times what these people want is to make money easily and quickly, but the truth is that this is not achieved through trading. That is why many people are constantly scammed by other people who claim that they have managed to accumulate huge fortunes by trading and that they can teach their techniques and secrets in exchange for a paid subscription or through some other service or product.

Don’t Fall into the Trap

Scammers often call themselves "mentors" or "teachers" who offer courses and programs that supposedly ensure people make a huge trading income in a short time. In general, these scammers find themselves flooding the internet with false information whose sole objective is to make people with little experience fall into that trap and buy those products that will only ensure that they lose money.

Most of the time, these scammers use social networks such as Instagram, Twitter, and Facebook to promote their fake products, just as they usually use a kind of pyramid scheme where people have to pay to enter a supposedly exclusive group where they will gain money in a very easy way, but the truth is that they end up losing their money.

Fake Mentorship Everywhere

Worst of all is that the number of these scammers has been increasing exponentially over time since they know that people have become much more interested in these topics in recent years. One of the easiest ways to spot a fake mentor is that they promise you incredible returns and tell you that there is no risk involved. Well, that is a pretty big red flag, since, in the world of trading, high returns are usually accompanied by a very high risk. Similarly, in a world as unpredictable as that of trading, it is impossible to ensure that a profit will be made with a trade, so we must try to stay away from those who want to buy us with those false promises. This means that there will be many people trying to offer you their help, advice, and even asking you for a commission in exchange for the promise of obtaining extremely high returns through the advice they give in social media groups or any digital platform

Build Your Road

Many times, people who know nothing (or know very little) about trading want a guide or series of methods that will ensure their success. However, trading is something that must be done on an individual basis, as not all people have the same goals or the same financial situation. That is why we must build our trading plan in a personalized way so that we can be successful traders.

That is why we should not compare our performance with other people or despair when we do not immediately get the results we want. Trading requires time, effort, dedication, and a lot of emotional intelligence, so we must focus on building our path and correcting as we go. Trading is based on the perseverance and discipline that we have, so if we stay constant with our operations and practice every day, we should have no doubts that we can become those successful traders that we want to be.

Chapter 5: The New Era of Traders

Trading has undoubtedly democratized finance today. This is because, currently, anyone can access this wonderful industry, unlike what happened in previous decades when online trading did not exist. At that time, to trade financial assets, people had to go to financial institutions or to their preferred bank to be able to carry out most of these operations.

In the same way, previously these institutions asked people a large number of requirements to open their positions, such as a huge minimum deposit amount, an excellent credit record, and that the person was linked to the top management of a company, to ensure that that person had financial solvency and that they could be granted the leverage that was needed to trade at that time. This is quite the opposite of what is currently happening, where everyone can open an account with an online broker for free, quickly, and easily.

Avoid Emotional Decisions

All the operations we carry out must be based on technical analysis. That is, all our decisions must be based on the analysis we have made of supply and demand, price charts, support and resistance lines, income statements of companies, or any other type of financial analysis. We must get as far as possible from the news that revolves around the world of finance, as well as the external noise that is often generated on some financial asset.

Many times, people make emotional decisions, and they are not based on any type of financial analysis. These decisions are usually extremely detrimental to the trader since they are far from the principles of trading that tell us that we should always make decisions only based on financial analysis. In the same way, we should never make decisions based on anger, sadness, frustration, or joy, since each of these emotions can cause us great losses when we try to recover a previous loss by investing overflowing amounts of money.

Everybody Wants a Piece of the Cake

There are very few methods that allow us to make money from home (or wherever we are) in a way as comfortable as trading. The problem is that many times people confuse that comfort with a lack of discipline, perseverance, and hard work. Of course, trading does not require physical effort like other jobs, but a lot of dedication must still be put into it if we want to be successful in this world.

Likewise, everyone wants to have a piece of the pie, since trading is an industry that moves billions of dollars every single day. We must not be fooled, but we must focus on educating ourselves as much as possible about trading so that we can become excellent traders and take control of our finances once and for all.

Conclusion

One of the biggest changes that the process of globalization and the information age has brought is that more and more people tend to seek innovative ways to make money. People are no longer satisfied with having only one income, since taking into account the historical events of the world economy, having only one income is very dangerous. Instead, people (especially young people) are using available technological resources to multiply their money, mainly using the tools provided by the stock market.

Trading gives us the opportunity to generate money from our home (or anywhere in the world) constantly and, also, in an entertaining way. With all the techniques that we have learned in this book, we will be able to optimize our trading strategy much more in order to obtain better returns in each of our operations.

Without a doubt, online brokers have come to the world to democratize the world of finance. This occurs since previously the stock market was totally centralized on Wall Street, and all operations had to go to a bank or a financial institution, which usually charge high commissions and many times end up representing a problem for small investors, since there are usually minimum investment amounts. On the other hand, with all the online brokers that we have available today, we have many financial operations just one click away, something that is extremely useful for both small and more experienced investors.

Of course, if we really want to take advantage of all the strategies and knowledge acquired through this book, we must have the necessary discipline to keep learning constantly. The problem many people have is that they are left with some basic concepts and forget to keep learning, and this is something very serious in the world of finance today, as it is a very dynamic and changing world. Instead, by staying up to date with all the topics pertinent to trading, we will ensure that we stay ahead of all the new techniques and methods that will allow us to multiply our money even more.

In the same way, all this knowledge will be of no use if we do not apply it in real life later. Of course, since you have taken the time to read this book, I have no doubt that you are willing to continue learning and put all this knowledge into practice. While these techniques may be wrong sometimes, as no trader has achieved a perfect trajectory, being on this journey is about making mistakes, but we can learn from them and improve based on our previous experiences. Without a doubt, our financial future will be based on decisions we make in the present. What do you say? Are you ready to start your journey as a trader and start taking control of your financial life? If your answer has been yes (and I am sure that it was), then I must tell you that you have taken the main step towards financial freedom, and I'm really happy for that.

References

10 great ways to learn stock trading. (2017, March 29). StockTrader.com. https://www.stocktrader.com/learn-stock-trading/

Burns, S. (n.d.). *7 reasons to never give up trading*. New Trader U. https://www.newtraderu.com/2015/06/23/7-reasons-never-give-trading/

Commodities trading: An overview. (2019). Investopedia. https://www.investopedia.com/investing/commodities-trading-overview/

Stock trading: How to begin, how to survive. (n.d.). NerdWallet. https://www.nerdwallet.com/article/investing/stock-trading-how-to-begin

What is cryptocurrency trading and how does it work?. (n.d.). IG. https://www.ig.com/en/cryptocurrency-trading/what-is-cryptocurrency-trading-how-does-it-work

www.ingramcontent.com/pod-product-compliance
Ingram Content Group UK Ltd.
Pitfield, Milton Keynes, MK11 3LW, UK
UKHW021931200726
13853UKWH00010B/38

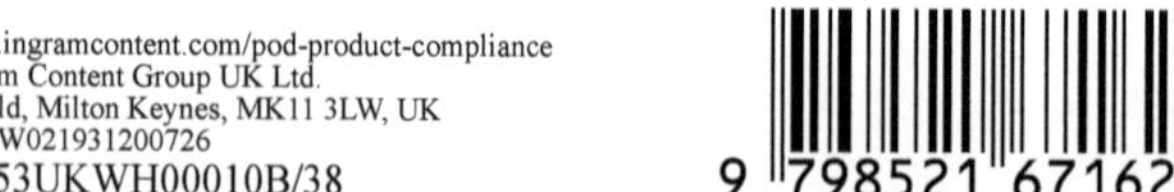

9 798521 671625